Copyright © 2016 CQ Products
Waverly, IA 50677
All rights reserved.
No part of this book may be reproduced or transmitted in any form or by any means, electronic or mechanical, including photocopying, recording or by any information storage and retrieval system, without permission in writing from the publisher.

Printed in the United States of America
by G&R Publishing Co.

Distributed By:

507 Industrial Street
Waverly, IA 50677

ISBN-13: 978-1-56383-426-4
Item #7132

5 JOYS OF 5 INGREDIENTS

1. You won't need to gather oodles and oodles of ingredients.
2. Fewer ingredients = less time-consuming cooking
3. Grocery shopping? Easier and less expensive!
4. Less prep means fewer dishes to clean!
5. Good food. Full stomachs. Happy people.

REJOICE!

Tip: *Make the most of your "5" by cooking with ingredients that are flavor- and ingredient-heavy, like O'Brien potatoes (with peppers and onions already included), frozen rice & vegetable blends, or canned tomatoes that already have herbs and spices inside.*

Serves 6-8

TOMATO-BASIL SOUP

4 C. tomato juice

4 medium tomatoes, peeled, seeded & diced

14 fresh basil leaves

1 C. heavy cream, plus more for serving

¼ to ½ C. butter, cut into pieces

1 Pour the tomato juice into a big saucepan and add the tomatoes. Simmer over medium heat for 30 minutes, stirring occasionally. Let cool a few minutes.

2 Carefully pour the hot tomato mixture into a blender and add the basil leaves; blend until pureed.

3 Warm 1 cup cream in a clean saucepan over very low heat. Gradually stir pureed tomato mixture into cream and stir in the butter. Warm the soup over medium-low heat until the butter melts, stirring often, without bringing it to a boil.

4 Season with salt and black pepper if you'd like, and swirl in a little more cream just before serving.

Toss on a few croutons for good measure. Serve with crusty bread to turn this comforting soup into a meal.

PIZZA CHICKEN SPIRALS

4 boneless, skinless chicken breast halves

Pepperoni slices

1½ C. shredded mozzarella cheese, divided

2 tsp. Italian seasoning

1 (15 oz.) jar pizza sauce

1. Preheat the oven to 350° and grease a 7 x 11" baking pan.

2. Pound each breast half to ¼" thickness. Top each chicken piece with a single layer of pepperoni, keeping it about ½" away from the edges. Sprinkle with black pepper if you'd like. Cover the pepperoni on each with about ¼ cup cheese and sprinkle with ½ teaspoon seasoning. Roll up each one tightly, tucking in edges, and secure with toothpicks.

3. Arrange the chicken rolls in the prepped pan and pour the pizza sauce over the top. Cover with greased foil and bake for 40 to 50 minutes or until the chicken is cooked through. Uncover, sprinkle with the remaining ½ cup cheese, and bake 5 minutes longer or until cheese is melted.

MAKES 4

ROASTED CORN-STUFFED TOMATOES

½ C. fresh sweet corn kernels
4 medium tomatoes
½ C. cooked quinoa
Garlic & herb seasoning blend
Shredded cheese *(we used smoked Gouda and farmer)*

1. Put the corn kernels in a dry skillet and set over medium-high heat. Cook and stir until the corn has browned nicely. Remove from the heat and set aside. Preheat the broiler.

2. Slice the tops off the tomatoes. Run a knife around the inside of the tomatoes, then carefully scoop out the insides. Put the scooped-out portion in a food processor and pulse until no large chunks remain; drain off excess liquid and dump the drained tomatoes into a bowl with the quinoa, seasoning, and set-aside corn. Season with salt and black pepper if you'd like. Add a small handful of cheese and stir to mix well.

3. Stuff the hollowed-out tomatoes with the quinoa mixture, mounding the top. Sprinkle additional cheese on top and set tomatoes in a muffin pan.

4. Broil 7" or 8" away from the heat for 3 to 5 minutes until heated through, moving the pan closer to the heat for the last minute or two to brown the tops.

These tomatoes are a yummy light meal and packed with goodness! A fresh basil garnish adds flair.

> SERVES 6

QUICK SALMON CAKES

- 2 (5 oz.) pouches skinless boneless pink salmon
- 1 (14.5 oz.) can diced tomatoes with basil, garlic & oregano, drained
- 1 C. lightly packed fresh spinach, coarsely chopped
- 1 egg
- ¾ C. dry Italian bread crumbs

1. Put the salmon into a bowl and flake it with a fork. Mix in the tomatoes, spinach, egg, and bread crumbs, and shape the mixture into six patties, ½" to ¾" thick.

2. Heat a little canola oil in a big skillet over medium heat. Add the patties and cook 4 to 5 minutes or until browned. Turn carefully and cook 4 to 5 minutes more, until heated through.

3. Remove from the skillet and drain on paper towels.

Serves 6

5-CAN VEGGIE SOUP

- 1 (14.5 oz.) can diced tomatoes
- 1 (15 oz.) can whole kernel corn
- 1 (15 oz.) can ready-to-serve vegetable or minestrone soup
- 1 (15 oz.) can mixed vegetables
- 1 (15 oz.) can black beans, drained & rinsed

1. Dump the tomatoes, corn, soup, mixed vegetables, and black beans into a big saucepan and give it a quick stir.

2. Warm the soup over medium heat and serve.

A DOLLOP OF SOUR CREAM ADDS A BIT OF CREAMINESS TO THE SOUP.

SERVES 4

SPAGHETTI CARBONARA

8 oz. uncooked spaghetti
2 eggs
¾ C. grated Parmesan cheese
4 bacon strips, cut into bite-size pieces
3 tsp. minced garlic

1. Cook the spaghetti according to package directions; reserve ¾ cup cooking water before draining. Meanwhile, whisk together the eggs and cheese. Set all aside.

2. Cook the bacon until crisp; drain on paper towels, keeping the drippings in the pan. Add the garlic to the drippings and heat for 1 minute, then reduce the heat to low. Quickly stir in the set-aside pasta, egg mixture, and bacon; toss gently. Season with salt and black pepper if you'd like.

3. Stir in the reserved pasta water a little at a time, until the mixture reaches the desired consistency. Serve immediately.

Easy on the cook. Yummy on the taste buds.

CRESCENT CALZONE BAKE

- 2 lbs. Italian sausage or lean ground beef
- 8 oz. sliced fresh mushrooms
- 1 (24 oz.) jar spaghetti sauce
- 2 (8 oz.) tubes garlic butter refrigerated crescent rolls
- 8 oz. fresh mozzarella cheese, sliced

1. Preheat the oven to 350°. Brown the meat, breaking it apart as it cooks and adding the mushrooms during the last few minutes of cooking; drain, return to the pan, and stir in the spaghetti sauce.

2. Press one tube of crescent rolls into the bottom of an ungreased 9 x 13" baking dish; seal seams. Spread the meat mixture evenly over the dough. Top with cheese and sprinkle with black pepper if you'd like. Unroll the remaining tube of crescent rolls over the ingredients in the pan without sealing seams.

3. Bake for 30 minutes or until the crust is deep golden brown and the filling is bubbly, covering with foil during the last few minutes of baking time to prevent overbrowning, if necessary.

THE QUICK WAY TO MAKE CALZONES.

SERVES 4

SPEEDY BEEF STIR-FRY

1 lb. sirloin steak
1 (14 oz.) pkg. frozen stir-fry vegetables, thawed
1 tsp. minced garlic
2 T. soy sauce
2 (3 oz.) pkgs. beef ramen noodles

1. Cut the steak into thin 2"-long strips. Heat a little vegetable oil in a big skillet over medium-high heat and add the beef strips. Cook until browned on both sides, turning once.

2. Move the beef toward the edge of the skillet and add the vegetables and garlic to the center; cook for 2 to 3 minutes, stirring vegetables constantly. Stir the beef into the vegetables and add soy sauce; cook 2 minutes longer or until the vegetables are tender.

3. Meanwhile, cook the noodles according to package directions, adding seasoning packets if you'd like; drain. Serve the meat and veggies over the noodles.

SPRINKLE WITH TOASTED SESAME SEED JUST BEFORE SERVING IF YOU'D LIKE.

Serves 4

SKILLET SAUSAGE ALFREDO

- 8 oz. uncooked pasta *(any type)*
- 1 (13 oz.) pkg. smoked sausage, sliced
- 2 C. heavy cream
- 2 tsp. Cajun seasoning
- ½ C. shredded Parmesan cheese

1. Cook pasta according to package directions; drain and set aside.

2. Meanwhile, toss the sausage into a big skillet and sauté several minutes until toasty-looking, stirring occasionally. Stir in the cream and seasoning; bring to a low boil. Reduce the heat and simmer for 5 to 8 minutes or until the mixture starts to thicken, stirring often. Stir in the cheese until melted. Add the set-aside pasta and toss lightly to coat.

MAKES 8

CRUNCHY FISH TACOS

8 frozen battered fish fillets or tenders *(about 2 oz. each)*

8 (6") corn tortillas

Shredded green cabbage

Black bean & corn salsa

Red onion

1. Bake fish according to package directions. Meanwhile, fry the tortillas one at a time in a little vegetable oil in a skillet over medium heat until just beginning to brown on one side. Flip the tortilla over and fold to form a taco shell; fry until golden brown and crispy on both sides. Transfer to paper towels to drain.

2. Fill fried shells with baked fish, cabbage, salsa, and onion.

TRY THESE WITH A BIT OF SOUR CREAM.

WHITE CHICKEN PIZZA

2 (6") prebaked pizza crusts

2½ T. garlic & herb butter spread

Provolone cheese *(6 large slices plus ¼ C. shredded)*

1 C. frozen popcorn chicken, thawed

Diced tomato

1. Preheat the oven to 450° and set the crusts on an ungreased baking sheet.

2. Melt the butter spread, drizzle it over the crusts, and spread it around evenly. Cover each crust with half the cheese slices. Cut the chicken into bite-size pieces and arrange over the cheese. Sprinkle the shredded cheese over the top.

3. Bake for 9 to 11 minutes or until cheese is melted and lightly browned. Top with tomato.

CHICKEN PARM WITH A TWIST

2 eggs
1¼ C. dry Italian bread crumbs
4 chicken breast halves (about 4 oz. each)
1 C. shredded Gouda cheese
Pizza sauce

1 Preheat the oven to 350°. Line a rimmed baking sheet with parchment paper and coat with cooking spray; set aside.

2 In a shallow bowl, beat the eggs and add salt and black pepper if you'd like. Put the bread crumbs in a separate shallow bowl. Dip both sides of each breast half first in the egg and then in the crumbs and arrange on the prepped baking sheet.

3 Lightly spritz the breaded chicken with cooking spray and bake for 20 minutes or until just cooked through. Remove from the oven, sprinkle each with half the cheese, and drizzle each with some pizza sauce. Bake an additional 10 minutes, until cheese is melted and sauce is hot.

Gouda cheese is a nice alternative to Parmesan. It's mild, creamy, and scrumptious.

Serves 6-8

CHEESY CHICKEN CASSEROLE

- 1 (10.5 oz.) can cream of chicken with herbs soup
- 1 (8 oz.) container sour cream
- 1½ C. shredded smoked cheddar cheese
- 1 (28 oz.) bag frozen diced O'Brien hash browns *(mostly thawed)*
- 3 C. chopped rotisserie chicken or leftover turkey

1 Preheat the oven to 350° and butter a 9 x 13" baking dish. In a big bowl, mix the soup, sour cream, and cheese until well combined. Stir in hash browns and chicken. Spread in the prepped baking dish and cover with foil.

2 Bake for 1 hour. Uncover; bake 15 minutes more, until bubbly. *(For crunch, add shoestring potatoes the last 15 minutes of baking time.)*

Serves 6

NACHO BEEF SKILLET

- 1 lb. lean ground beef
- 1 (14.5 oz.) can diced tomatoes with green chiles
- 1 (11 oz.) can Mexicorn, drained
- 1 (5.25 oz.) box Spanish rice mix *(ready in 10 minutes)*
- 1½ C. shredded Mexican cheese blend

1. Brown the meat in a big skillet, breaking it apart as it cooks; drain and return to the skillet. Stir in the tomatoes, corn, rice mix, and 1½ cups water. Bring to a boil over medium-high heat; cover, reduce heat to medium, and cook for 3 minutes. Remove from the heat and let stand, covered, for 8 minutes or until the rice is tender.

2. Sprinkle the cheese over the food in the skillet and let stand until melted.

ONE PAN RANCH DINNER

4 bone-in pork chops (about ¾" thick)

1 lb. new red potatoes, quartered

1 lb. fresh green beans, trimmed

1 (1 oz.) pkg. dry ranch salad dressing mix

1½ tsp. minced garlic

1. Preheat the oven to 400° and spritz a large rimmed baking sheet with cooking spray.

2. Set the pork chops on the prepped baking sheet and arrange potatoes and beans around them. Drizzle everything with a little olive oil and sprinkle with the salad dressing and garlic; season with salt and black pepper if you'd like.

3. Bake for 20 minutes or until the veggies are crisp-tender and the chops reach an internal temperature of 140°. Turn on the broiler and broil for 3 or 4 minutes until caramelized, browned, and the internal temperature reaches 145°.

THIS MEAL BAKES TOGETHER IN ONE PAN. IT COULDN'T BE EASIER!

Serves 4

Serves 4

PECAN-COCONUT TILAPIA

½ C. finely ground raw coconut chips
½ C. finely chopped pecans
½ tsp. red pepper flakes
2 eggs
4 (4 oz.) tilapia fillets

1. In a shallow bowl, combine the coconut, pecans, pepper flakes, and salt if you'd like; mix well. In another shallow bowl, whisk the eggs.

2. Heat about 2 tablespoons oil in a big skillet over medium heat. Working in batches, dip the fish in eggs to coat both sides, then coat with the coconut mixture, patting well to help coating stick. Fry two fillets at a time for 2 to 3 minutes on each side or until crust is lightly browned and fish flakes easily with a fork.

Serve with roasted veggies for a quick meal that's sure to please.

Serves 4

TORTELLINI SOUP

2 (32 oz.) cartons chicken broth
1 (10 oz.) pkg. julienned or shredded carrots
½ (19 oz.) pkg. frozen cheese tortellini
½ C. sliced celery
1 C. frozen peas

1. In a big saucepan, bring the broth to a boil. Add carrots, tortellini, celery, and a little black pepper if you'd like; return to a boil.

2. Cook uncovered for 7 to 9 minutes or until the tortellini is tender, adding the peas during the last few minutes of cooking time.

Serves 6

BBQ PORK & APPLES

- 4 C. cooked & shredded pork roast
- 1 C. smoky BBQ sauce
- ⅓ C. frozen apple juice concentrate
- 1 lg. apple, cored & sliced (try Rome, Gala, or McIntosh)
- ½ tsp. cinnamon-sugar

1. Combine the pork, BBQ sauce, and juice concentrate in a saucepan; heat until warm, stirring often.

2. Meanwhile, melt a little butter in a skillet over medium heat. Add the apple along with the cinnamon-sugar and cook for 5 to 6 minutes or until tender, stirring constantly. Serve the pork and apples together on buns if you'd like.

Yummy with coleslaw (see page 60).

Serves 6

TERIYAKI ONION BURGERS

- 1½ lbs. lean ground beef
- ¼ C. plus 2 T. teriyaki sauce, plus more for brushing
- 1 (3 oz.) can French fried onions, crushed
- 6 hamburger buns, split
- 2 C. shredded green cabbage

1. Grease the grill grate and preheat the grill on high heat. Mix the meat, ¼ cup plus 2 tablespoons teriyaki sauce, and French fried onions; shape into six patties.

2. Grill patties for 5 minutes on each side or until done to your liking, brushing with more teriyaki sauce occasionally. Spritz cut sides of buns with cooking spray and grill until toasted.

3. Serve burgers and cabbage on toasted buns.

SIMPLE, SUPER JUICY, AND UTTERLY DELICIOUS.

RAVIOLI LASAGNA

- 2 (24 oz.) jars marinara sauce
- 2 (25 oz.) pkgs. frozen sausage ravioli, thawed
- 1 (16 oz.) jar roasted red peppers, drained & chopped
- 1 (8 oz.) pkg. shredded mozzarella cheese
- ½ C. shredded Parmesan cheese

1 Preheat the oven to 400° and coat a 9 x 13" baking pan with cooking spray; set aside.

2 Spread half the marinara sauce from one jar in the prepped pan. Arrange half the ravioli over the sauce, top with half the peppers, and spread the remaining sauce from the first jar over the top. Sprinkle with half the mozzarella and half the Parmesan. Repeat the layering with the remaining sauce, ravioli, peppers, and mozzarella. Set the remaining Parmesan aside.

3 Cover with greased foil and bake for 35 minutes. Uncover and bake an additional 15 minutes or until the cheese is melted and the sauce is bubbly. Remove from the oven and sprinkle with the remaining Parmesan.

Layer upon layer of flavor—with no preboiling noodles!

SERVES 8

Serves 2

CHICKEN TACO BAKE

2 boneless, skinless chicken breast halves
Taco seasoning to taste
½ each red and green bell pepper
½ onion
¾ C. shredded Mexican cheese blend

1. Preheat the oven to 375°. Arrange breast halves in a greased 8 x 8" baking dish and sprinkle with as much taco seasoning as you like.

2. Slice up the peppers and onion and arrange the slices over the chicken; drizzle with a little water or olive oil. Then just sprinkle on the cheese and bake for 35 to 45 minutes or until the chicken is cooked through.

Serve over rice, or slice the chicken and wrap everything in flour tortillas if you'd like.

Serves 3

GREEN CHILI CHICKEN ENCHILADAS

- 1¼ lbs. boneless, skinless chicken thighs
- 1 (28 oz.) can green enchilada sauce
- 1 (5.75 oz.) can whole green chiles, drained
- 6 (8") flour tortillas
- 1 (8 oz.) pkg. shredded Pepper Jack cheese

1. Preheat the oven to 400° and coat a 9 x 13" baking pan with cooking spray.

2. Heat 2 tablespoons olive oil in a big skillet. Add chicken and cook for 4 minutes on each side. Add ¼ cup water, scraping up any browned bits from the bottom of the pan. Add the enchilada sauce and bring to a simmer; cover and cook over medium-low heat for 20 minutes, until chicken is cooked through. Remove the chicken pieces and shred into a bowl. Set all aside.

3. Set a dry skillet over medium-high heat. Toss in the chiles and heat until lightly charred on both sides, turning once; chop into bite-size pieces and stir into the shredded chicken. Spread the mixture evenly down the center of the tortillas, sprinkle each with 2 tablespoons cheese, and roll up tightly. Place seam side down in prepped pan.

4. Pour the set-aside sauce evenly over the enchiladas, sprinkle with the remaining cheese, and season with salt and black pepper if you'd like.

5. Cover the pan with greased foil and bake for 20 minutes. Uncover and bake 5 minutes longer or until hot and bubbly.

MIX SOUR CREAM WITH ENOUGH MILK TO THIN IT; DRIZZLE OVER THE ENCHILADAS AND TOSS ON A HANDFUL OF CILANTRO. GARNISH COMPLETE.

SEAFOOD PAELLA EXPRESS

- 1 (10 oz.) pkg. frozen rice & vegetable blend *(we used Southwest-style rice with corn, peppers & onions)*
- 1 tsp. ground turmeric
- ½ lb. fresh sea scallops
- ½ lb. cooked shrimp, peeled & deveined, thawed if frozen
- 2 Roma tomatoes, coarsely chopped

1. Prepare the rice blend according to package directions; transfer to a serving bowl and stir in turmeric.

2. Meanwhile, in a medium skillet, heat a little vegetable oil over medium heat. Add scallops and cook for 3 minutes or until opaque. Add the shrimp and tomatoes and heat through.

3. Using a slotted spoon, transfer the seafood and tomato mixture to the bowl with the rice; toss to combine. Season with salt and black pepper if you'd like.

Fresh herbs go with just about every dish—we tossed on a bit of parsley here.

SERVES 4

VEGGIE-CHORIZO QUICHE

- 1 (9 oz.) pkg. ground chorizo sausage
- 10 eggs, divided
- 4 lg. sweet potatoes, peeled & shredded
- 2 C. lightly packed fresh spinach, coarsely chopped
- ½ red bell pepper, chopped

1. Preheat the oven to 350°. Brown the meat in a deep 12" oven-safe skillet, breaking it apart as it cooks; remove the meat with a slotted spoon, drain, and set aside.

2. Whisk 2 eggs in a medium bowl. Add the sweet potatoes and mix well; press into the bottom and up the sides of the same skillet, creating a crust. Bake for 35 to 40 minutes, until the edges are slightly brown. Remove from the oven and set aside. Increase the oven temperature to 375°.

3. Whisk the remaining 8 eggs with 1 cup water until well blended. Stir in the spinach and bell pepper; season with salt and black pepper if you'd like.

4. Pour the egg mixture over the crust, sprinkle with the set-aside meat, and bake for 35 to 40 minutes, until the middle is set. Let stand 10 minutes before cutting.

These ingredients blend to create a wonderful flavor combo!

FLANK STEAK PINWHEELS

⅔ C. sun-dried tomatoes *(not packed in oil)*

1 lb. flank or flat iron steak, trimmed

2 tsp. minced garlic

3 T. bacon- or jalapeño-flavored cream cheese spread

1 C. lightly packed fresh spinach, coarsely chopped

1. Place the tomatoes in a bowl and cover with boiling water. Let stand for 10 minutes or until softened; drain, finely chop, and set aside.

2. Grease a grill rack and preheat the grill on high.

3. Meanwhile, pound the meat to ¼" thickness and rub garlic all over both sides. Spread the cream cheese in a 3"-wide lengthwise strip down the center of the meat. Cover the cream cheese with the spinach and top with the set-aside tomatoes.

4. Starting at one long edge, roll up the meat tightly, tucking in the filling as you go. Sprinkle the outside of the roll with salt and black pepper if you'd like. Push eight evenly spaced toothpicks through the roll, catching the edge of the meat to help hold in the filling. With a sharp knife, cut the roll between each toothpick to create eight equal pinwheels.

5. Grill several minutes on each side, until done to your liking, turning carefully. Let rest 5 minutes before serving.

The filling in these pinwheels adds mouth-watering flavor to the steak. Serve 'em hot off the grill for instant gratification!

Serves 6

ZESTY SHRIMP & RICE

- 2 (10 oz.) pkgs. frozen rice & vegetable blend *(we used Steamfresh brown & wild rice with corn, carrots & peas)*
- 1½ lbs. raw jumbo shrimp, peeled & deveined
- 1 lemon, cut into wedges
- 1 (.7 oz.) pkg. dry Italian salad dressing mix
- ½ C. melted butter

1. Preheat the oven to 425° and grease a 9 x 13" baking pan. Dump in the rice blend, shrimp, and lemon.

2. Mix the salad dressing and butter and pour over the food in the pan; stir to coat and spread out evenly. Cover the pan and bake about 30 minutes or until the shrimp just turn pink, stirring lightly once during baking.

MAKES 4

LOADED SWEET POTATOES

- 4 sweet potatoes
- 1 sweet onion, sliced
- 2 red bell peppers, cut into strips
- 1 or 2 green chile peppers, chopped
- 2 C. frozen burger-style crumbles *(such as MorningStar Grillers Crumbles)*, thawed

1 Preheat the oven to 350° and line a baking sheet with foil. Rub the sweet potatoes with vegetable oil, pierce several times with a fork, and bake on the prepped baking sheet about an hour, until tender.

2 Meanwhile in a big skillet, sauté the onion, bell peppers, and chili peppers in a little vegetable oil for 15 minutes or until very tender, stirring in the crumbles during the last few minutes. Serve over split baked sweet potatoes.

Serves 4

CREOLE CHICKEN CORDON BLEU

- 4 boneless, skinless chicken breast halves
- 1 tsp. Creole seasoning, more or less to taste
- 6 slices Swiss cheese, divided
- 1 (3 oz.) pkg. sliced prosciutto
- ½ C. crushed French fried onions

1 Preheat the oven to 350° and coat a 7 x 11" baking pan with cooking spray.

2 Pound each breast half to ¼" thickness and sprinkle with seasoning. Place one cheese slice on each and cover with prosciutto. Roll up and secure each with a toothpick.

3 Arrange the chicken rolls in the prepped pan. Sprinkle evenly with crushed onions, pressing firmly to adhere. Bake for 35 to 40 minutes or until chicken is cooked through. Remove from the oven, place ½ cheese slice on top of each roll-up, and bake a few minutes more, until cheese has melted.

Tastes great served with pasta salad (see page 60 for an easy 5-ingredient recipe).

MAKES 6

BBQ BEEF CUPS

1 lb. lean ground beef
¾ C. chopped onion
1 C. BBQ sauce
1 (12 oz.) tube refrigerated Texas-style biscuits
1½ C. shredded cheddar cheese

1 Preheat the oven to 400°. Lightly grease six jumbo muffin cups.

2 Brown the meat and onion together in a skillet, breaking it apart as it cooks; drain and return to the skillet. Stir in the BBQ sauce and simmer for a few minutes, until heated through.

3 Separate the biscuits and roll each one out on a floured surface to 6" in diameter. Press each biscuit into the bottom and up the sides of a prepped muffin cup.

4 Divide the cooked meat mixture evenly among the cups and sprinkle with the cheese. Bake 12 to 15 minutes or until the biscuits are nicely browned.

Grab a beef cup and some fruit and you've got yourself a meal.

CHILI-BROILED FISH & VEGGIES

¼ C. mayo
1½ tsp. chili powder
4 pollock fillets
1½ C. frozen corn kernels, thawed
1 pint cherry tomatoes, cut in half

1. Preheat the broiler. In a small bowl, mix the mayo and chili powder; spread a thin layer of this mixture on the bottom of a 7 x 11" metal pan. Arrange the fillets on top and sprinkle with salt and black pepper if you'd like. Spread the remaining mayo mixture over the fish.

2. Dump the corn evenly over the fish and scatter the tomatoes over the top.

3. Broil 6" from the heat about 15 minutes or until the tomatoes are slightly charred and the fish is cooked through.

Toss together a quick green salad and your meal is ready in a flash.

Serves 4

Serves 4

CURRY CHICKEN & RICE

- 1 (7.2 oz.) pkg. rice pilaf mix
- 1 tsp. curry powder
- 2 C. shredded rotisserie chicken
- 1 (14.5 oz.) can diced tomatoes with green chiles
- 1 C. frozen peas

1. Pour 1¾ cups water and 1 tablespoon olive oil into a big saucepan and bring to a boil. Stir in pilaf mix and its seasonings; add the curry powder and return to a boil. Then reduce the heat, cover, and simmer for 15 minutes.

2. Stir in the chicken, tomatoes, and peas. Cook, covered, 8 to 10 minutes longer or until liquid is nearly absorbed and rice is tender. For a little crunch, toss on some cashews before serving.

MAKES 4

ALFREDO POTATOES

4 large baking potatoes
1 (8 oz.) pkg. sliced fresh mushrooms
3 C. lightly packed fresh spinach, coarsely chopped
1 (14.5 oz.) jar Alfredo sauce
1 Roma tomato, diced

1. Preheat the oven to 350° and line a baking sheet with foil. Rub the potatoes with vegetable oil; sprinkle with coarse salt and black pepper if you'd like. Pierce several times with a fork and bake on the prepped baking sheet about an hour, until tender.

2. Heat a little butter in a skillet; sauté the mushrooms until softened. Add the spinach; cook until just wilted, stirring constantly. Stir in the Alfredo sauce, bring to a simmer, and cook 5 minutes until slightly thickened. Serve over split baked potatoes and top with tomato.

SERVES 4

BLONDE FRENCH DIPS

1 (11 oz.) tube refrigerated French bread

1 red onion, thinly sliced

1 (14.5 oz.) can chicken broth

¾ to 1 lb. thinly sliced deli turkey

4 to 6 oz. Brie cheese, sliced

1 Preheat the oven to 350°. Coat a large cookie sheet with cooking spray and set the dough on it, seam side down. With a serrated knife, cut six diagonal ½"-deep cuts on top of the loaf and sprinkle with coarse black pepper if you'd like. Bake for 22 to 26 minutes or until golden brown; set aside.

2 Sauté onion in about 2 tablespoons olive oil over medium heat for 2 minutes. Stir in the broth and turkey, season with salt and black pepper if you'd like, and bring to a boil. Cook 2 to 3 minutes more, until onion is tender.

3 Cut bread loaf crosswise into four equal pieces and slice each piece in half horizontally. Place cheese slices on bread. Fill each sandwich with turkey and onions, reserving the broth for dipping.

THE SCENT OF BAKING BREAD WILL BRING THE FAMILY TO THE TABLE; THE TASTE OF THESE SANDWICHES WILL KEEP THEM THERE.

FAJITA-STYLE PORK KABOBS

8 baby red potatoes

1 lb. pork tenderloin, cut into 1" pieces

1 (1.4 oz.) pkg. fajita seasoning mix

1 bell pepper, any color, cut into 1" pieces

1 medium onion, cut into 1" pieces

1. Put the potatoes and 3 tablespoons water in a covered microwaveable bowl; microwave for 4 minutes or until nearly tender.

2. Put the tenderloin and seasoning in a bowl and stir until coated. Alternately thread meat, potatoes, bell pepper, and onion onto skewers.*

3. Grease the grill grate and preheat the grill on medium-high heat. Arrange the kabobs on the grill, close the lid, and cook for 10 minutes or until pork is cooked through, flipping halfway through cooking time. Brush kabobs with a little vegetable oil as needed to moisten.

*If using wooden skewers, soak them in water for 30 minutes or use metal skewers.

FOR ADDED ZIP, SET OUT SOME LIME WEDGES FOR SQUEEZING JUICE OVER THE KABOBS.

5-INGREDIENT SIDES

Quick Coleslaw

Whisk together 1 C. mayo, 2 T. sugar, 2 T distilled white vinegar, ½ tsp. celery seed, and ½ tsp. salt *(optional)*. Stir in 1 (16 oz.) pkg. shredded coleslaw mix. Serve immediately or chill first.
Serves 6

Garden Pasta Salad

Cook 2 C. garden rotini pasta in boiling water to al dente following package directions; rinse in cold water and drain well. Combine the pasta, ½ C. diced bell pepper *(any color)*, 6 sliced cherry tomatoes, and ¼ C. sliced Kalamata olives. Drizzle with enough Italian dressing to moisten. Cover and refrigerate until serving time.
Serves 4

Summer Chop Salad

Combine 2 diced tomatoes, 1 diced cucumber, and 2 peeled and diced avocados. Stir in ¼ chopped red onion, and 3 to 4 T. lime vinaigrette. Season with salt and black pepper if you'd like. Garnish with a little crumbled feta cheese, or skip the onion altogether and use ⅓ C. crumbled feta in its place. **Serves 4**

Three Bean Salad

Combine 1 (15 oz.) can three bean salad, 2 diced Roma tomatoes, ½ C. diced red onion, 2 T. chopped fresh cilantro, and ¼ C. lemon herb vinaigrette. Toss well, cover, and refrigerate until serving time. **Serves 4**

5-INGREDIENT DESSERTS

Key Lime Cups

Beat 1 (8 oz.) pkg. softened cream cheese with 1 (14 oz.) can sweetened condensed milk, ½ C. key lime juice, and the zest of 1 lime until smooth. Divide evenly among six dessert dishes and top each with about 1 T. graham cracker crumbs. Garnish with whipped topping and more lime zest if you'd like. **Serves 6**

Chocolate Puffs

Thaw one sheet frozen puff pastry; cut along fold lines and cut each strip into four squares. Bake at 400° for 15 minutes, until golden; cool. Melt together ¾ C. mini marshmallows, 3 (1.55 oz.) milk chocolate candy bars *(broken)*, and ¼ C. milk; cool. Beat 1 C. heavy cream until nearly stiff; stir into chocolate mixture. Split pastries and fill with chocolate. **Makes 12**

Cherry Crescents

Preheat the oven to 375° and line a baking sheet with parchment paper. Unroll 1 (8 oz.) tube refrigerated crescent rolls and arrange individual crescents on the parchment; place 1 T. cherry pie filling on the wide end of each and roll up. Bake 9 to 12 minutes, until golden. Mix ½ C. powdered sugar, ½ tsp. almond extract, and enough milk to thin; drizzle over warm crescents. **Makes 8**

Peach Cobbler

Preheat the oven to 375° and grease a 9 x 13" baking pan. Drain 2 (29 oz.) cans sliced peaches; spread in the prepped pan. Mix 1 C. milk and 1 C. each sugar and self-rising flour; whisk in ½ C. melted butter until blended. Pour batter over peaches; don't stir. Bake 40 minutes or until browned and bubbly. *(Can replace self-rising flour with 1 C. all-purpose flour, 1½ tsp. baking powder, and ¼ tsp. salt.)* **Serves 8**

INDEX

5-Can Veggie Soup 11
Alfredo Potatoes 55
BBQ Beef Cups 50
BBQ Pork & Apples 31
Blonde French Dips 56
Cheesy Chicken Casserole 24
Cherry Crescents 63
Chicken Parm with a Twist 22
Chicken Taco Bake 36
Chili-Broiled Fish & Veggies 52
Chocolate Puffs 62
Creole Chicken Cordon Bleu 48
Crescent Calzone Bake 14
Crunchy Fish Tacos 19
Curry Chicken & Rice 54
Fajita-Style Pork Kabobs 58
Flank Steak Pinwheels 44
Garden Pasta Salad 60
Green Chili Chicken Enchiladas 38
Key Lime Cups 62
Loaded Sweet Potatoes 47
Nacho Beef Skillet 25
One Pan Ranch Dinner 26
Peach Cobbler 63
Pecan-Coconut Tilapia 28
Pizza Chicken Spirals 6
Quick Coleslaw 60
Quick Salmon Cakes 10
Ravioli Lasagna 34
Roasted Corn-Stuffed Tomatoes 8
Seafood Paella Express 40
Skillet Sausage Alfredo 18
Spaghetti Carbonara 12
Speedy Beef Stir-Fry 16
Summer Chop Salad 61
Teriyaki Onion Burgers 32
Three Bean Salad 61
Tomato-Basil Soup 4
Tortellini Soup 30
Veggie-Chorizo Quiche 42
White Chicken Pizza 20
Zesty Shrimp & Rice 46